"What a felicitous title for Meehan's latest book! Each chapter opens with an appropriate scriptural quotation, moves on to help us reflect on it, and concludes with prayer exercises. Christians, whether busy or not, will find this book extremely helpful not only to realize how God takes delight in them but also to take delight in God."

Peter C. Phan
Professor of Systematic Theology
Catholic University of America

"Some of us would like to know God's 'delighting' more personally and more often. And not just believe it—rather dimly, from a distance. In *God Delights in You*, Bridget Meehan wants to move readers from the what and why to the *who* and *how*.

"Hers is real spiritual exercise—unfolding from the traditional and transitional—on the way to not-yet and still-more. It is updating without outdating healthy stems from the past. Here, 'a fundamental shift in thinking' is evolving and involving. Us.

"The author presents Delight's ever-new wisdom as a practiced art, designed to be moving. Her use of experience is state-of-the-art. I find particular delight in the women of scripture chosen as prophets of healing in our time and space."

Mary Lou Sleevi
Artist and author, *Sisters and Prophets*,
and *Women of the Word*

"Are the spiritual manuals today coming out of the management field? Many of these texts deal with governing values, the search for balance, vision, and mission statements. None of them invites us to contemplative prayer in order that we might discover God's infinite love, encounter divine mercy, experience deep healing, live lives of empowerment.

"Bridget Mary Meehan's four-week prayer journal for busy Christians—*God Delights in You*—does offer that invitation and she provides a detailed methodology. Be careful! A serious working with this text could transform your life."

Robert F. Morneau
Auxiliary Bishop of Green Bay

"Sr. Bridget knows how to pray. In *God Delights in You*, she opens the way for busy people to enter into a new intimacy with God. By means of reflection, relaxation, and journaling, she guides the reader to a deeper level of prayer. The increased sense of God's love then empowers the pray-er to share that love with the community, the church, and society.

"For anyone seeking the grace of God for physical or emotional healing, I particularly recommend the third chapter. Beyond oneself, the reader is led in healing prayer for planet Earth and for victims of injustice."

Rev. Lynn Johnson
Presbyterian Church (USA)

A Four-Week Prayer Journal
for Busy Christians

GOD DELIGHTS IN YOU

Bridget Mary Meehan

TWENTY-THIRD PUBLICATIONS
Mystic, Connecticut 06355

Twenty-Third Publications
185 Willow Street
P.O. Box 180
Mystic, CT 06355
(203) 536-2611
800-321-0411

ISBN 0-89622-603-4
Library of Congress Catalog Card Number 94-60352
Printed in the U.S.A.

Dedication

To my family:
my parents, Bridie and Jack,
my aunt Molly McCarthy,
my brothers, Patrick and Sean,
my sisters-in-law, Valerie and Nancy,
my niece, Katie, and nephew, Danny

To all my Irish relatives: Noreen and Ger Davy and their children, Brendan and Louise; Aunt Peg and Uncle Jack Meehan; Molly Meehan; John and Mary Meehan and their children, Eoin, Elaine, and Clare; Seamus Meehan; Margaret and Aidan Ryan; Mary and Allan Tregent and their son Darren; Mary and Bernie Ferns and their children, Brian, Shane, and Darren; Pat and Eileen Meehan and their children, Ruth and James; Sean and Alice Meehan and their children, James, Brian, Sean, Avril, Elaine, Bill, Niall, Colm, Orla, and Matthew; Esther Meehan; Paddy Meehan; Kathleen and Desmond McNamara and their children, Adrian and Desmond; Tim and Rose Meehan and their children, Roy, John, Miriam, and Katherine; Tess and John Murphy and their children, Elizabeth and Katherine.

Acknowledgments

I am grateful for the support of good friends and members of the small faith communities at Fort Myer, Virginia, who have shared their wisdom, love, and support with me over the years, especially Irene Marshall, Jeanette Kraska, Daisy Sullivan, Ana Minassian, Phyllis and Wendall Hurst, Dennis and Sue Wenzel, Ray and Carol Buchanan, Peg and Bob Bowen, Donna Mogan, Mary Jo Grotenrath, Bill and Marie Dillon, Elizabeth Hoisington, Dick and Mary Guertin, Lynn Johnson, Larry Skummer, Mike Marshall, Maria Billick, Michal Morsches, Debbie Dubuque, Doris Mason, Patricia Herlihy, Paul and Shirley Hurley, Judy and Frank Dillon, Jack Doyle, Mary Kay and John Salamone, Fritz and Barbara Warren, Sr. Roseanne Fedorko, Sandra Voelker, John Weyand, Helen Groff, Millie Nash, Francis L. Keefe, Joseph Mulqueen, Michael Pollitt, Regina Madonna Oliver, and Mary Emma Hadrick.

Contents

God Delights in You

Introduction

How do we discover God's infinite love in our lives?
What does it mean to be aware of God dwelling within
our spiritual depths? How does God's love liberate,
heal, transform, and empower us? Do we desire to encounter a God who delights in us and "can accomplish
abundantly far more than all we can ask or imagine"?
(Ephesians 3:20) Are we willing to risk everything for so
great a love?

   In *God Delights in You: A Four-Week Prayer Journal for
Busy Christians*, I draw on the rich tradition of the scriptures and the writings of the Christian mystics to help
readers enter into and experience God's extravagant
love. This journal invites you to contemplate your experiences of the depths of God's love. It offers new possibilities for encounters with the God who loves each
one passionately, boundlessly, beyond all hopes and
dreams. Through the techniques of imaginative and cen-
tering prayer, together with spiritual journaling as an in-
tegrating exercise, you will be guided to enter more
deeply into God's love for you and experience the power of that love by exploring these themes:

   Week One: Discovering God's Infinite Love
   Week Two: Encountering Boundless Mercy
   Week Three: Experiencing Deep Healing
   Week Four: Living Our Empowerment

   This journal invites you to discover the power of
God's love and challenges you to be a contemporary
mystic in the real world. It offers creative suggestions

and practical ways to contemplate the God who delights in you. It is an ideal resource for small faith communities who want to enter into, experience, and share God's transforming love with others.

By creating a deeper awareness of God's tremendous love in the ordinary events of life, *God Delights in You* prepares you to reflect on your experiences of being loved by God and to grasp fully, in the words of St. Paul, "the breadth and length and height and depth, and to know the love of Christ that surpasses knowledge, so that [we] may be filled with all the fullness of God" (Ephesians 3:18-19).

When you use this tool for contemplation each day, when you sit in quiet with your God, when you share your insights with others, when you encounter the stress-filled demands of contemporary life, I pray that your ever-growing delight may be the discovery of how deeply God delights in you.

WEEK ONE

Discovering God's Infinite Love

Prayer is a journey to the center of our being where God dwells. There we can experience the inbreaking of God's love in every area of our lives. God loves each of us as if each person is the only one in existence. When we live at the center with God, all our joys, laughter, tears, sufferings, successes, losses, strengths, failures, indeed all of life become moments when we are embraced by God.

This means that we need more than an intellectual understanding that God loves the unique persons we are. It means that we need to experience this love on a feeling level. Somewhere, somehow we need to feel God's passionate, tender love liberating, healing, transforming us in the deepest levels of our beings. We need to reflect on the power of this love in the ordinary events of our everyday lives.

These reflections in Week One give us an opportunity to enter into the heart of God and to listen to God's personal words of love directed to each of us: "I love you." "You are precious to me." "I will never forget you." "I delight in you." Through scripture and the experiences of Christian mystics, we explore profound revelations of God's love for us. There we discover rich glimpses into the splendor of God's love and the impact that these new experiences of divine love have on our lives.

This section begins by introducing us to a God who passionately loves us. "God is love and those who abide in love abide in God, and God abides in them" (1 John 4:16). Then we listen as God speaks intimately to our hearts: " . . . you are precious in my eyes and glorious and I love you" (Isaiah 43:4). The image of motherly tenderness in the following passage reveals God's nurturing love for us: "Can a mother forget her infant, be without tenderness for the child of her womb? Even should she forget, I will never forget you" (Isaiah 49:15). Aware that God always delights in us, we can hope for our future because: "God will rejoice over you with gladness, [and] renew you . . . in love" (Zephaniah 3:17).

As we reflect on our past, we discover that even in our mother's womb, God's love has been with us: "Truly you have formed my inmost being, you knit me in my mother's womb . . . " (Psalm 139:13). Medieval mystic Mechtild of Magdeburg[1] reveals a rich glimpse of a God who sings us a love song:

> God takes such delight in the human person that Divinity sings this song to our soul: O lovely rose on the thorn! O hovering bee in the honey! O pure dove in your being! O glorious sun in your setting! O full moon in your course! From you I your God will never turn away.

Teresa of Avila, sixteenth-century reformer and Doctor of the Church, invites us to open ourselves to the fullness of divine love in our lives: "O Love that loves me more than I can love myself or understand."[2]

Discover God's love in new and powerful ways in the following meditations!

WEEK ONE
Day One

God is love
and those who abide in love
abide in God,
and God abides in them.

1 John 4:16

Reflections

1. The scriptures proclaim a God who passionately loves us. Recall a time in your life when you experienced God's love. In what ways have you grown spiritually because of this experience?

2. Reflect on all the ways you now experience God's love in your life.

3. Is there some area(s) in your life in which you really need God's love in a special way?

4. How can you become more aware of God's love in your life?

Prayer Experiences

1. Breathe slowly and deeply.

2. Be aware that God loves you completely and passionately. Picture God's love for you as a warm, soothing bath. As you breathe in, imagine God's gentle love flowing over you, washing away anxiety and stress. As you breathe out, imagine God's love cleansing and healing you.

3. Reflect on the following affirmation: God is deeply in love with me. Pray this affirmation as a mantra or prayer phrase through the day as a reminder of God's intimate love. Pray this affirmation—God is deeply in love with (name)—for family, friends, community, church, and world.

4. Be aware of any desires you have for a deeper intimacy with God. Ask God to tenderly embrace you with the fullness of divine love.

5. Imagine God loving you as you have never been loved before. What is God's love like? How did God "feel" toward you? How did you feel? Wonder? Joy? Gratitude? Awe?

6. Invite God to free you of any blockages that keep you from being receptive to God's love in your life.

7. Spend time contemplating and celebrating the breadth and length and height and depth of God's love for you and how much God wants to give you the gift of Self. Imagine yourself "acting as if" such a love is at the heart of all your relationships and activities. Be conscious of any new insights, feelings, images, thoughts, that emerge from this awareness.

WEEK ONE
Day Two

. . . you are precious
in my eyes and glorious
and I love you.

Isaiah 43:4

Reflections

1. What experiences of being profoundly loved have you had in your life? In what ways are you changed because of them?

2. Do you believe that God affirms you at this moment and loves you with boundless love?

3. Do you see yourself as a person worthy of God's love? What obstacles keep you from seeing yourself as precious and glorious in God's eyes?

4. How does it feel to be loved and affirmed by God? What difference can this experience make in your life?

Prayer Experiences

1. Take some time to relax your body and find a comfortable place in which to rest. Close your eyes. Let go of any stress or tension. Become conscious of God's presence deep within you and all around you.

2. Reflect on the relationships you have had with people who have loved you deeply. Recall them one by one. How have you experienced love in these relationships? What impact did these loving relationships have on your life? How are you different now because of these relationships? Share your responses with God.

3. In God's presence, reflect on the following questions: Do I feel loved by God? In what ways has God affirmed me? What obstacles keep me from seeing myself as a lovable person?

4. Listen to God say to you, "(your name), you are precious in my eyes and glorious, and I love you." Imagine God naming some special qualities that you have.

5. Imagine God repeating these affirmations over and over, especially as you face obstacles, fears, and anxieties. How would you feel? Can you share your reaction with God?

6. Create your own mantra to remind you of God's immense love for you. A mantra is a prayer that consists of seven syllables or fewer. One form of mantra is a breath prayer. Breathe in on the first three syllables and breathe out on the last three. The middle syllable is the breath change between breathing in and out.

7. Pray one or more of the following mantras to remind you each day of God's love:

My love will never leave you.
You are my beloved.
I will love you forever.
I embrace you with my love.

Day Three

Can a mother forget her infant,
be without tenderness for the child of her womb?
Even should she forget,
I will never forget you.

Isaiah 49:15

Reflections

1. How does this image of motherly tenderness reveal new insights into God's love for us?

2. In what ways do you need God to nurture you now?

3. What thoughts, images, feelings, insights does the image of God as tender mother stir within you? Do you find this image helpful in understanding more deeply the mystery of God's love?

4. How can you help others experience God's nurturing love in their spiritual lives?

Prayer Experiences

1. Be still. Breathe deeply. Relax your entire body. Imagine relaxation flowing through your body from head to toe. Focus on each area and imagine your body letting go of tension and becoming completely relaxed.

2. Imagine yourself as a mother even if you are a man. Begin with the moment of conception. Then reflect on your pregnancy and the birth of your baby. Imagine how you would feel as you held your infant in your arms for the first time.

3. Now imagine God as a nurturing mother holding you close to her breasts. Allow God to caress and kiss you. Invite God to minister to your deepest needs. Ask God to free you from worry and anxiety; to liberate you from compulsions and sin; to heal you physically, emotionally, spiritually; and to empower you with the courage you need to live as a holy and whole person.

4. Nothing can separate us from God's nurturing love, not even sin. Contemplate God's mothering love that has been always there for you, especially during times of failure and weakness. God is like a tender mother who strengthens us in our struggles to overcome evil. In your verbal prayers today, remember all people who struggle with the forces of evil throughout the world.

5. Ask God to reveal to you ways you can share God's love with others. Do something for someone today that would be an expression of God's motherly love for them.

6. During the day today reflect on this scripture verse: Can a mother forget her infant, be without tenderness for the child of her womb?

Even should she forget,
I will never forget you.
Isaiah 49:15

Be aware of any thoughts, images, feelings, insights, sensations, and memories that God's love stirs within you.

7. Record your insights, feelings, thoughts, images, sensations, memories in a journal, in poetry, art, song, dance, or in any other creative way.

WEEK ONE
Day Four

God . . . will rejoice over you
with gladness,
(and) renew you in . . . love.

Zephaniah 3:17

Reflections

1. As you reflect on your life at the present time, what are you joyful about? How do you see God being revealed to you in this joyful situation?

2. Was there ever a time when you were vividly aware of God delighting in you? If so, what was that awareness like for you? If not, what do you think that would be like for you?

3. Now reread Zephaniah 3:17. How does it make you feel to realize that God rejoices over you and renews you in love? How can you become a more joyful person?

4. What can you do to celebrate life?

Prayer Experiences

1. With both of your feet on the floor and your hands comfortably on your lap, close your eyes. In the stillness, focus on your breathing. Feel the air as it moves in and out of your nostrils. Focus simply on being in love with God.

2. During this prayer time, open yourself to the joy in the heart of God. Contemplate God creating, nurturing, and loving you during the different stages of your life. If you wish, write down the important moments in your development, beginning with conception up to the present. Allow yourself to focus upon feelings, images, and impressions that come to you about being loved and cherished by God during these times.

3. Imagine God rejoicing over you, singing a love song to you, shouting your praises to all creation, and dancing for joy because of you. Reflect on the impact that such an image of God would have on your life. Reflect on the impact that such an image of God would have on how other people see themselves, others, Earth, the cosmos.

4. Compose a psalm or litany of thanksgiving expressing your gratitude for God's love for you.

5. Rejoice with God in the goodness and beauty of Earth. Marvel at the connectedness and interdependence of life as God created it. Observe God delighting in the sun . . . moon . . . planets . . . stars . . . Earth . . . water . . . fire . . . animals . . . plants . . . flowers . . . trees . . . human beings. Ask God to help you appreciate and celebrate all

of Earth's creatures. Decide on one thing you can do to make Earth a more beautiful place to live.

6. Pray for those who are sad, lonely, and depressed. Ask God to help you identify ways you can minister to someone in need of encouragement and love.

7. Plan to do something today to celebrate life: take a walk, soak in a hot bath, breathe deeply, smell a flower, look at the sunset, visit a friend, read poetry, sing and dance, listen to children laugh, etc.

WEEK ONE
Day Five

Truly you have formed my inmost being;
you knit me in my mother's womb.
I give you thanks that I am fearfully, wonderfully made;
wonderful are your works.
My soul also you know full well;
nor was my frame unknown to you
when I was made in secret,
when I was fashioned in the depths of Earth.
Your eyes have seen my actions;
in your book they are all written;
my days were limited before one of them existed.
How weighty are your designs, O God;
how vast the sum of them!
Were I to recount them,
they would outnumber the sands;
did I reach the end of them,
I should still be with you.

Psalm 139:13–18

Reflections

1. As you reflect on God forming you in your mother's womb, what images, feelings, insights, sensations, or memories occur to you?

2. As you reflect on God shaping your life now, what images, feelings, insights, sensations, or memories occur to you?

3. How can you become more aware of your identity as a beautiful reflection of God's image?

4. What can you do to become more conscious of God's wondrous love in the ordinary events of your life?

Prayer Experiences

1. Become relaxed and still. Be aware of your breathing. Inhale and exhale slowly, allowing God's relaxing love to permeate your entire being. Picture tension being replaced by relaxation, in your head, face, neck, shoulders, chest, back, arms, hands, fingers, hips, stomach, legs, feet, toes.

2. In your imagination, form a picture of God embracing you in your mother's womb. Open yourself to the depths of God's tender love forming and shaping you. Imagine God declaring you in all your uniqueness—body, mind, spirit—wonderful, beautiful.

3. Now imagine God looking at you now as you are, with boundless love. Allow this love to saturate your entire being. Listen to God tell you how much you are loved.

4. Be aware of any feelings, insights, thoughts, sensations, images that emerge as you reflect on God's love for you. Share these in a prayerful dialogue with God.

5. Ask God to help you be more attentive to God's awe-filled love for you in the ordinary events of your day (for example, breathing, eating, listening, talking, walking, sleeping, etc.). Take a moment each time you are about to do this activity to recall that God is present, loving you, filling you, renewing you, inspiring you, refreshing you, etc.

6. Give thanks that you are wonderfully made. You are God's special creation—a work of art—with unique gifts and qualities that reflect the divine image. God is

present to you, loving you every moment of every day.

7. In silence, spend some time reflecting on any new insights you discovered about God's love for you during your prayer today.

Day Six

From the very beginning
God loved us.
The Holy Trinity
gave itself
in the creation of all things
and made us
body and soul,
in infinite love.
We are fashioned most nobly.

God takes such delight in the human person
that Divinity sings this song to our soul:
O lovely rose on the thorn!
O hovering bee in the honey!
O pure dove in your being!
O glorious sun in your setting!
O full moon in your course!
From you
I your God
will never
turn away.[3]

Mechtild of Magdeburg

Reflections

1. What is God revealing to you about divine love in this meditation of Mechtild of Magdeburg? What impact might this have on your relationship with God?

2. How are you presently involved in bringing God's tender love to others?

3. How can Christians be a sign of God's love for the world?

4. What can you do today to help others experience God's nearness in their lives?

Prayer Experiences

1. When you are relaxed, calm, and conscious of God's loving presence, imagine a breathtaking scene from nature such as a beautiful sunrise, a star-studded sky, a vibrant rainbow, lovely wildflowers, a bubbling creek, a diving eagle, a newborn robin. Notice the details, the colors, the textures, the shapes.

2. As you inhale, be aware of God's love embracing all of creation and filling your entire being with joy and peace. As you exhale, let go of all negativity, fear, and anxiety. Do this exercise for several minutes or until you feel centered.

3. Become conscious of being in the presence of God always. Every sight you see, every sound you hear, everything you taste, smell, and touch can be opportunities for meditating on the divine presence in all of life. Every person you meet reflects God's image and is potentially an encounter with the Holy One.

4. If you are near a window, look out and be aware of all you see. Use your senses to get in touch with the marvels of creation outside your window. Praise God for everything you see, hear, smell, touch, taste.

5. Throughout the day, be conscious that you are seeking God's will first in everything that occurs. Reflect on your priorities in life and how you feel about them. Be aware that you are one of God's favorite dwelling places. Who you are as well as what you do gives glory to God.

6. In your journal, compose a litany, song, dance, or poem of thanksgiving for God's closeness to you. Or draw or paint a symbol or image of God's profound love for you.

7. Decide on some practical act of service you can do to help others experience God's nearness in their lives.

WEEK ONE
Day Seven

O Love that loves me more
Than I can love myself or understand![4]

Teresa of Avila

Reflections

1. What are the major obstacles that keep you from loving yourself?

2. How can you open yourself to the fullness of God's love now?

3. What can you do to share God's love with people you find difficult to love?

4. How have you helped others to be more receptive to God's love in their lives?

Prayer Experiences

1. In the stillness, become aware of God's extravagant love in your life.

2. In your imagination, form a picture of God embracing you. Open yourself to the fullness of God's love for you. Allow this love to permeate your entire being.

3. Invite God to reveal to you any area in your life in which you need to feel divine love.

4. Consider your doubts and uncertainties. Ask God to be with you in times of pain and darkness. During your prayer, open your hands and surrender each of these areas or situations to God. Be receptive to all that God wants to do for you.

5. Begin a prayerful dialogue with God about one of these areas. Share your thoughts, feelings, anxieties, joys, fears, or anger with God. Listen to God's response. Realize that this dialogue may go beyond words. You may experience God's love healing you in new and powerful ways.

6. Be aware of anyone in your life you find difficult to love. Share your feelings about this person with God. Imagine God holding this person close to the divine heart. Listen as God speaks loving words to this person. Now imagine God holding both of you close to the divine heart. Open yourself to whatever God wants to do to heal this relationship. Ask God to help you see the other person and yourself with loving compassion.

God's love with this person. Ask God to give you opportunities to share the liberating, healing power of
God's love with others, especially those who are lonely,
depressed, isolated, or alienated.

WEEK TWO

Encountering
Boundless Mercy

The Hebrew word for mercy, *rachamim*, is derived from the word *rechem*, which means womb. According to this beautiful image, mercy comes from God's womb-love which warmly embraces us with tenderness when we come laden with sin and guilt.

In both Hebrew and Greek languages, wisdom is feminine, the feminine dimension of the one God and is personified as Sophia. In his poem, "Hagia Sophia" Thomas Merton reflects: "Sophia is the mercy of God in us, the tenderness with which the infinitely mysterious power of pardon turns the darkness of our sins into the power of grace."[5]

"Mercy is interwoven with forgiveness," observes Patricia Livingston in *Lessons of the Heart*.[6] Jesus showed us the power of merciful forgiveness from the cross in his conversation with a convicted criminal. One condemned man humbly acknowledged his past failures as he spoke to the other criminal: "'And we indeed have been condemned justly, for we are getting what we deserve for our deeds, but this man has done nothing wrong.' Then he said, 'Jesus, remember me when you come into your kingdom.'" Jesus revealed the tender mercy of God in his reply, "Truly I tell you, today you will be with me in Paradise" (Luke 23:41–43).

The mercy of forgiveness lifts the burdens of guilt and shame from our shoulders. A friend of mine once confided that she had not spoken to her brother because of a family squabble several years ago. Then one day it dawned on her how much she missed him.

All of a sudden I realized that life is so short and love is all that matters. I called Tom on the phone, told him that I was sorry for the things I said and did that hurt him. My brother was so touched that his voice choked up as he told me how much he missed and loved me. After we reconciled I felt like a weight had been lifted from my heart and I experienced a deep peace.

An inability to forgive others can cause physical and emotional illnesses. These problems often are rooted in hostilities, resentments, bitterness, and unresolved conflicts. These situations disrupt people's well-being and cause disorders such as headaches, exhaustion, backaches, sleeplessness, ulcers, and other symptoms of stress. In these situations forgiveness is often one of the significant factors that helps the body and mind let go of guilt and pain, and experience healing.

A divorced father recently complained about problems with anxiety and depression.

I guess I never forgave my wife for walking out on me and leaving me with a small child. But the other day when I looked at my little girl and saw her mother's smile, I knew what mercy felt like. It was hard but I prayed for the first time: God, help me to really want to forgive my wife.

The reflections in Week Two invite us to encounter God's mercy in new and powerful ways. Through scripture and the experiences of Christian mystics, we discover that God always takes the first step to embrace us with the tenderness of divine mercy. The parable of God the extravagant Father told in the gospel of Luke (15:11–32) reveals a God who is always ready to forgive us, no matter how often, or how seriously we have sinned.

The prophet Hosea describes God's mercy as the quality that touches us most deeply in our brokenness: "I will heal their defection, I will love them freely (14:5)." Psalm 103 reveals healthy ways of dealing with guilt and shame in our lives. Did you ever feel lost? Is there a part of you that needs to be freed, healed, transformed? If so, take courage. God, like the woman who turned her house upside down looking for a lost coin, will never give up on you until she finds you. The Peace Prayer of St. Francis encourages us to be gentle and merciful with self and others. In Julian of Norwich's *Showings*, we contemplate the light of divine mercy shining in the darkness and our own and the world's suffering. The revelation of God's merciful love for all generations found in Mary's Song of Praise (Luke 1:46–55) challenges us to live a simpler lifestyle, to look for fresh perspectives, and to find innovative approaches to address some of the pressing ecological issues of our times: limiting our excessive consumption of resources such as food, water, trees, clothing, electricity, fuel, etc.

Encounter God's boundless mercy embracing you and all creation in the following meditations!

Week Two
Day One

"Father I have sinned against heaven and against you.
I no longer deserve to be called your son;
treat me as you would treat one of your hired workers."
So he got up and went back to his father.
While he was still a long way off,
his father caught sight of him,
and was filled with compassion.
He ran to his son, embraced him and kissed him.

Luke 15:18–20

Reflections

1. This parable reminds us that the love of God is like that of a merciful, extravagant father who is always ready to forgive. How does it make you feel that God is always ready to forgive you, no matter how much you have sinned or turned away from divine love?

2. What is God revealing to you about God's immeasurable love in this story?

3. What feelings arise in you when you reflect on God's forgiving love present with you in your sinfulness, weaknesses, and vulnerability?

4. How can Christians be signs of God's tender mercies to the world?

Prayer Experiences

1. Breathe slowly and deeply. Relax your body by releasing any stress you feel in your muscles. Move from the top of your head to the soles of your feet, alternately tightening and relaxing the muscles in each area of your body.

2. Read the story of the loving father in Luke 15:20–24.

3. Be aware that God loves you with a unfathomable love. Picture yourself as one of the characters in the parable above: the forgiving father, the prodigal son, or the elder son. As you do so, be aware of your feelings and reactions. Be attentive to what God has revealed to you. Record in your journal any insights, images, thoughts, perspectives that emerge.

4. Be aware of any area of sin, weakness, or brokenness in which you need forgiveness and healing. Invite God to free you from any fears or anything else that keeps you from being receptive to God's mercy. Ask God to embrace you in this area with the fullness of divine love.

5. Observe God forgiving, liberating, healing, and transforming you in the area in which you felt the greatest guilt and shame. Be conscious that God delights in you even though you are imperfect. How did God "feel" toward you? How did you feel? Wonder? Joy? Gratitude? Awe?

6. Pray for victims of oppression, discrimination, and abuse, and for those who oppress others, discriminate against others, and abuse others. As you pray, imagine

God forgiving, liberating, healing, and empowering each person and group.

7. Imagine yourself "acting as if" you are a forgiven and forgiving person in all your relationships with others. What difference would this make? What difference would it make if all Christians were to act this way? Be conscious of any new insights, feelings, images, thoughts that emerge from this awareness.

WEEK TWO
Day Two

I will heal their defection,
I will love them freely.

Hosea 14:5

Reflections

1. What experiences of being forgiven have you had in your life? In what ways are you changed because of them?

2. Do you see yourself as a person in need of God's forgiveness? What obstacles keep you from seeing yourself as sinful, wounded, imperfect?

3. Do you believe that God desires to heal you at this moment and embrace your wounds with boundless mercy?

4. How does it feel to experience God's forgiving love? What difference can this experience make in your life?

Prayer Experiences

1. Close your eyes. Spend at least five minutes being completely still. In the silence, become conscious of God's mercy surrounding you.

2. Reflect on the relationships that you have had with people who have loved you deeply. Recall them one by one. Have you experienced giving and receiving forgiveness in these relationships? How are you different now because of these relationships? Share your responses with God.

3. In God's presence, reflect on the following questions: How have you failed to love God and others? What sinful choices have you made recently that damaged self and/or others? What consequences have these sinful choices had?

4. Confess your sins to God. Ask God to heal any inner attitudes that keep you from loving God and others.

5. Be aware of any specific areas in your life that may need God's healing. Ask God to embrace you in each of these areas.

6. Listen to God speak you name and say, "(your name), I will heal your defection. I will love you freely."

7. Create your own mantra to remind you of God's forgiveness and healing love. A mantra is a prayer that consists of seven syllables or less. One form of mantra is a breath prayer. Breathe in on the first three syllables and breathe out on the last three. The middle syllable is the breath change between breathing in and breathing out.

WEEK TWO
Day Three

Bless God, O my soul,
and all that is within me,
bless Yahweh's holy name.
Bless God, O my soul,
and do not forget Yahweh's benefits—
who forgives all your iniquity,
who heals all your diseases,
who redeems your life from the Pit,
who crowns you with steadfast love and mercy,
who satisfies you with good as long as you live
so that your youth is renewed like the eagle's.

Psalm 103:1–5

Reflections

1. How do you react when you experience blame, shame, or guilt in your life?

2. Why is it important to find healthy ways of dealing with guilt and shame?

3. What is God revealing to you about divine mercy in this psalm that could help you deal with guilt and shame in your life?

4. What can you do today to be an instrument of God's mercy to those who experience guilt and shame in their lives?

Prayer Experiences

1. Sit in a relaxed position with your eyes closed or focused on a familiar symbol, such as a candle, a cross, a painting, the sky, trees, flowers, birds, water. Be aware of your breathing.

2. After a few minutes of quiet relaxation, slowly read the psalm.

3. Recall a time in your life when you experienced guilt or shame. As you remember the situation, reflect on how you felt and acted. Did you blame yourself or others for what happened?

4. Ask God to reveal the fears and anxieties that keep you from opening yourself more deeply to God. Observe yourself surrendering these fears one by one to God. Imagine God freeing you from guilt and healing you totally. Allow the warmth of that love to fill your heart with peace, joy, confidence, and with whatever you need to grow spiritually in the situation or relationship.

5. Observe the power of God's overflowing mercy to change how you now see this situation or relationship. See God giving you the strength you need to live as a new creation: fully alive and in love with God and others.

6. Pray Psalm 103 as a reminder that God's steadfast mercy has freed and healed you.

7. Be aware of anything you feel called to do as a result of your prayerful encounter with God's mercy.

WEEK TWO
Day Four

Or what woman having ten silver coins,
if she loses one of them,
does not light a lamp, sweep the house,
and search carefully until she finds it?
When she has found it,
she calls together her friends and neighbors, saying,
"Rejoice with me, for I have found the coin that I had lost."
Just so, I tell you,
there is joy in the presence of the angels of God
over one sinner who repents.

Luke 15:8–10

Reflections

1. Did you ever feel lost? Is there a part of you that needs to be freed, healed, transformed? Is there an area of your life in which you feel powerless and need to empowered?

2. From this passage of scripture and your reflections upon it, what did you learn about God's desire to find you?

3. How does this parable remind you that God always searches for us when we are lost—no matter how far we have strayed away—and desires only to find us?

4. Recall a time in your life when you discovered you were valuable to yourself, others, and God. Reflect on one or more of the following areas of your life:

when you learned to listen, understand, or love yourself, others, and God.

when you worked for equality, justice, and peace in our world.

when you affirmed your strengths and identified your weaknesses.

when you became confident about your identity.

when you served others generously and compassionately.

when you focused on your spiritual and professional growth.

when you learned to eat nutritious meals, rest, exercise, recreate.

Prayer Experiences

1. Be still and focus on your breathing. Feel the air as it moves in and out of your nostrils. Allow yourself to relax completely in God's loving presence for several minutes.

2. After your quiet time, read the story Jesus told (Luke 15:8–10) to describe God's mercy.

3. Close your eyes and visualize God as a woman looking for a lost coin in her home. Observe her moving the furniture around, anxiously looking under beds, tables, rugs, searching every drawer, closet, and cabinet. Experience her excitement when she finds her precious treasure and dances around the room with joy. Be aware that she invites friends, neighbors, and you to a gala celebration. What images do you see? How do you feel? Are you aware of any new insights into God's persistent mercy?

4. Be aware that God desires to heal and transform any area in your life or any part of you that is lost, wounded, or broken. Surrender each of these areas into the boundless heart of God's mercy. Observe God embracing you close to the divine heart, redeeming, healing, and transforming you. See yourself as a more glorious reflection of God's image.

5. Compose a psalm, song, painting, dance, or litany that expresses your gratitude for God's mercy in your life. Thank God for special times of growth in your life when you discovered that you were valuable to yourself, others, and God. Some possible themes for this work of praise are:

when you learned to listen, understand, or love yourself, others, and God.

when you worked for equality, justice, and peace in our world.

when you affirmed your strengths and identified your weaknesses.

when you became confident about your identity.

when you served others generously and compassionately.

when you focused on your spiritual and professional growth.

when you learned to eat nutritious meals, rest, exercise, recreate.

6. Ask God to help you identify ways you can minister to someone or to some group that feels powerless, alone, lost, or afraid.

7. Plan to do something today to celebrate God's desire to find affirm, heal, and transform you and the person or group you identified in #6.

Day Five

Lord, make me an instrument of your peace,
where there is hatred, let me sow love,
where there is injury, pardon,
where there is doubt, faith,
where there is despair, hope,
where there is darkness, light,
and where there is sadness, joy.

O, Divine Master, grant that I may not so much seek
to be consoled as to console,
to be understood as to understand,
to be loved as to love.

For it is in giving that we receive;
it is in pardoning that we are pardoned;
and it is in dying that we are born to eternal life.

Saint Francis of Assisi

Reflections

1. As you reflect on the Peace Prayer of St. Francis, what images do you have of yourself as a peaceful, gentle, forgiving person?

2. In what ways have you been self-abusive? Have you abused your body by eating or drinking too much? By taking drugs? Have you been cruel to yourself? Criticized, judged, or put yourself down?

3. In what ways has this self-abuse led to abuse of others?

4. In what ways can you be more gentle with self and others?

Prayer Experiences

1. In the stillness, immerse yourself in the tender mercies of God as you would a warm soothing bath of water. Soak in the comforting gentleness of God's love for you.

2. Imagine God telling you all about your goodness, your gifts, your beauty, your virtues. What thoughts, feelings, sensations, insights, images emerge when you reflect on God's boundless love for you? You may find it helpful to journal this conversation.

3. Be aware of ways you have been cruel to yourself by abusing your body through eating, drinking to excess, or taking drugs. Be conscious of times you have been too self-critical or occasions when you have driven yourself by too much work, activity, pressures.

4. Ask God for the gift of gentleness and mercy. Be aware of ways you can "lighten up" on self-criticism and self-abuse. Decide on one way you will practice the art of loving yourself in a healthy, wholesome way each day.

5. Be aware of times that you have been too demanding or abusive with family, friends, co-workers, neighbors, etc. Write down the names of several significant persons you have abused. Choose one of them to dialogue with—perhaps someone with whom you have had a difficult relationship or someone with whom you want to develop a closer relationship. Close your eyes and imagine yourself with this person. Begin to talk to this person about your desire for reconciliation or a closer relationship. Discuss what kinds of changes need

to occur before either or both of you will experience new life.

6. Imagine God filling you with a new gentleness toward this person. See yourself accepting, encouraging, affirming this person with their gifts and weaknesses as a beautiful image of God in your life. See yourself acting as a peaceful, strong, caring, gentle reflection of God's compassionate mercy in all your relationships.

7. Think of ways to celebrate this person's goodness. Choose to do something loving for this person. As you conclude your prayer time, slowly and meditatively, pray the Peace Prayer of St. Francis.

Day Six

Our faith is a light, coming in nature from our endless day,
which is our Father, God.
In this light our Mother, Christ, and the Holy Spirit
lead us in this passing life.
This light is measured with discretion,
and it is present to us in our need in the night.
The light is the cause of our life,
the night is the cause of our pain and all our woe,
in which woe we deserve endless reward and thanks from God;
for we by his mercy and grace
willingly know and believe our light,
walking therein wisely and mightily.
And at the end of woe, suddenly our eyes will be opened,
and in the clearness of our sight, our light will be full,
which light is God, our Creator, Father, and the Holy Spirit,
in Christ Jesus our savior.
So I saw and understood
that our faith is our light in our night,
which light is God, our endless day.[7]

Julian of Norwich

Reflections

1. What did you learn about our need for faith in God's saving power from this text?

2. Recall a particular time in your life when God was working to help you see light even in darkness, although you may not have been aware of it at the time.

3. What can you learn from that experience about what God may be doing in the present to bring light in the darkness and suffering of the world?

4. How can you share the light of God's mercy with others, the church, society, the world?

Prayer Experiences

1. Take time to be still and relax. As you inhale, breathe in the saving power of God. As you breathe out, breathe out any darkness within that keeps you from experiencing God's love. Repeat one of the following words or phrases for several minutes slowly and quietly: "God," "Jesus," "loving mercy," "healing light," "saving power," "redeeming presence." If you become aware of a distraction, simply let it go, and continue to repeat your prayer word or phrase. Simply "be" in God's grace-full presence.

2. Light a candle and reflect on God's mercy as the light shining in your darkness. Be aware of any areas of darkness within, any inner blockages to God's peace, love, freedom, any areas in which you need to experience redemption. Feel the purifying light of God's saving love transforming each area of darkness within you with forgiveness and healing.

3. As you meditate on this experience, what new understandings of God are you aware of? Share your thoughts, feelings, insights, images with God in a prayerful dialogue.

4. Reflect on times when you have experienced God's redeeming power bringing others, the church, society, the world out of the darkness into the light. If you would like, write a conversation between you and God about any one of these situations.

5. Read what you have written in this dialogue. What thoughts, feelings, insights, sensations do you experience? Express in words, impressions, or pictures anything you are aware of.

6. Draw a picture of yourself doing something to help others—the church, society, the world—encounter God's merciful love.

7. Be aware of any actions, choices, commitments you can make now to be a reflection of God's saving love for others. Make a list of "I can . . . " statements sharing what you have decided to do to share the light of God's merciful love with others in the church, society, the world.

Week Two
Day Seven

And Mary said,
My soul proclaims the power of God
and my spirit delights in God's wondrous ways,
for God has looked with favor on me.
All generations will call me blessed;
for God has done marvellous deeds for me,
Holy is God's name.
God's mercy embraces all people, all creation,
Earth and universe
from generation to generation.
God silences the proud in their inmost thoughts
with the strength of God's arm.
God puts down powers and principalities
and empowers the poor and oppressed;
God feeds the hungry while those who are full
leave empty-handed.
God has revealed mercy through all ages to our mothers and
fathers, grandparents, great grandparents,
according to the promise
God made to our ancestors in times past, now and forever.

Luke 1:46–55 (adapted)

Reflections

1. How can the revelation of God's merciful love from Mary's Song of Praise help you, your family, community, neighborhood, or the church address some of the pressing ecological issues of our times? (limiting excessive consumption of such resources as food, water, trees, fabrics, electricity, fuel; choosing a simpler lifestyle; fasting; abstaining; etc.)

2. How does material addiction and overconsumption keep society from empowering the poor and oppressed? What impact does over-consumption of material things have on your life?

3. How can you transform our wounded planet into a more healthy place? In what ways can working with others who are interested in environmental action help us to become agents of God's mercy to heal Earth?

4. What can you do to challenge unjust structures, liberate the poor and oppressed, engage in environmental action, live a simpler lifestyle so that others may simply live?

Prayer Experiences

1. In the stillness, become aware of God's merciful love for all creation. Look outside at nature or at a picture of nature for a few minutes.

2. In your imagination, form a picture of God embracing you, all creatures, the whole Earth. Open yourself to the fullness of God's overwhelming love for all creation. Imagine this love protecting, freeing, healing, transforming all creation. See all creatures and human beings as one family living together in peace and harmony, reverencing Earth as our sacred home.

3. Ask God to help you discern a way of living more simply, such as recycling, car-pooling, conserving heat and water, sharing excess food and clothing with the needy, making, rather than buying, Christmas, birthday, or anniversary gifts.

4. Pray each day for Earth and its endangered species.

5. Take a nature walk and praise God for each flower, tree, plant, animal, etc., that you see. Take deep breaths as you walk. Feel the warmth or coolness of the air, touch the rocks, ground, soil with reverent awe. Hug a tree. Look with love at the people you meet. Be aware of the goodness of God's creation and your responsibility to be a compassionate caretaker of Earth.

6. Reflect on the needs of the poor and oppressed people in the world. Image yourself working with God and others to challenge unjust structures and create a new world where justice, equality, and peace flourish. Be aware of any images, words, feelings, or insights that emerge.

7. Be aware of any decisions you can make now to challenge unjust structures, liberate the poor and oppressed, participate in environmental action to heal Earth, simplify your lifestyle.

WEEK THREE

Experiencing Deep Healing

In our journey of faith, all of us are concerned about healing . The experiences of physical illness, emotional pain, or spiritual struggle reveal our brokenness, emptiness, weakness, and the need for deep healing in our lives.

I still remember the panic I felt almost twenty years ago as if it was only yesterday when my doctor told me that I had a growth on my vocal cords. In order to permit my vocal cords to heal, my doctor recommended that I refrain from speaking for a month. As an extroverted person who loves to talk, I wondered how I'd ever survive a month of silence. But to my surprise I discovered that this was one of the most fruitful times of spiritual growth. I read books on healing, listened to tapes on inner healing, and prayed for healing.

As I sat outside on the patio each day bathed in the warm sunshine, I would image God's healing love flowing through my entire being. I imagined Jesus embracing me and healing not only my vocal cords but my fears of cancer and death. At the end of the month, not only had my vocal cords healed but my spiritual life had been enriched. I experienced God's love liberating, healing, transforming, touching every aspect of my life. I felt other people's pain more deeply. This led me to a ministry of intercessory and inner healing prayer. I found a new sense of peace about my future, a quiet realization that no matter what happened, all would be well.

The reflections of Week Three invite us to experience the deep healing of God in our lives. Through scripture and the experience of Christian mystics we discover that God saves, heals, and loves us always. The prophet

Isaiah (35:5–6) describes a time when all illnesses will be healed: "Then the eyes of the blind shall be opened, and the ears of the deaf unstopped; then the lame shall leap like a deer, and the tongue of the speechless sing for joy."

Jesus applied Isaiah's words to himself: "The Spirit of the Lord is upon me, because God has anointed me to bring good news to the poor. God has sent me to proclaim release to the captives and recovery of sight to the blind, to let the oppressed go free, to proclaim the year of God's favor." Jesus' healing ministry, a significant dimension of his ministry as Messiah, demonstrated that the reign of God was breaking forth in the world. The healings of Jesus reveal that the saving power of God is present among us.

Many of Jesus' encounters with women are healing stories. The woman with a twelve-year hemorrhage who touches Jesus' clothes in public reveals a woman's dignity as a person (Mark 5:25–34). The issues involved in this story go beyond healing the woman to the liberation of the community from taboo and exclusion. Jesus observes the grief of the widow of Nain, has compassion on her, tells her not to weep, and raises up her son (Luke 7:11–15). The healing of Peter's mother-in-law demonstrates the relationship between healing and service: "The fever left her, and she began to serve them" (Mark 1:30–31).

Jesus came to save us from fear and anxiety. Often our stress, fear, guilt, or sadness comes from root problems, from hurts, wounds, or conflicts we are not conscious of. We can pray to be healed of all that blocks us from being the loving individuals God calls us to be. In prayer we can invite Jesus to heal our deepest fears and wounds and fill us with peace. We can open ourselves to receive the gift Jesus wants us to give us: "Peace I leave with you, my peace I give to you. I do not give to you as the world gives. Do not let your hearts be troubled, and do not let them be afraid" (John 14:27).

Hildegard of Bingen, a twelfth-century theologian and mystic, challenges us to heal and be healed by Earth. For Hildegard, healing is the return of greening power and moistness. "The soul is the freshness of the flesh, for the body grows and thrives through it, just as Earth becomes fruitful through moisture."[8]

Meister Eckhart, a fourteenth-century Dominican preacher and theologian, believed that the heart of the spiritual journey is compassion. For Eckhart, compassion means healing interwoven with justice. In Eckhart's words: "The first of God's works is compassion . . . and the highest work of God is . . . compassion." Compassion means doing for others. We are to give birth to compassion by doing justice and relieving the suffering of others. According to Eckhart, "Your entire life will be called healed when you have entered into compassion and its works of justice."[9]

Open yourself to experience deep healing in your relationships with yourself, others, Earth, creation, God in the following prayer reflections.

Week Three
Day One

Strengthen the weak hands,
and make firm the feeble knees.
Say to those who are of a fearful heart,
Be strong, do not fear!
Here is your God.
Then the eyes of the blind shall be opened,
and the ears of the deaf unstopped;
then the lame shall leap like a deer,
and the tongue of the speechless sing for joy.

Isaiah 35:5–6

When Jesus came to Nazareth, where he had been brought up,
he went to the synagogue on the sabbath day,
as was his custom.
He stood up to read,
and the scroll of the prophet Isaiah was given to him.
He unrolled the scroll
and found the place where it was written:

The Spirit of the Lord is upon me,
because God has anointed me
to bring good news to the poor.
God has sent me to proclaim release to the captives
and recovery of sight to the blind,
to let the oppressed go free,
to proclaim the year of God's favor.

And he rolled up the scroll,
gave it back to the attendant, and sat down.
The eyes of all in the synagogue were fixed on him.
Then he began to say to them,
"Today this scripture has been fulfilled in your hearing."

Luke 4:16–21

Reflections

1. Isaiah reminded his listeners that God would heal all diseases. Jesus' words echoed Isaiah's insights about the importance of healing as a sign of God's power. Jesus' healing ministry, a significant dimension of his ministry as Messiah, demonstrated that the reign of God was breaking forth in the world. What does the healing ministry of Jesus reveal to you about God's presence in the world?

2. How have you experienced the healing presence of God in your life?

3. As you look at the life of your family, friends, and community of faith, is there a need for healing? Describe the need.

4. What is it that makes you feel afraid or anxious in your relationship with God at the present time?

Prayer Experiences

1. Slowly take a breath. Breathe again a little bit more deeply. Breathe slowly and deeply for a couple of minutes until you feel relaxed.

2. Become aware that the Good News of Jesus is important for our lives now. Jesus has come to release our total selves from the bondage of sin. He can heal our negative memories, attitudes, and behavior patterns.

3. Become conscious that Jesus has been ministering to you, loving, protecting you, liberating you, healing you, transforming you at every moment of your life. He has been present as savior in every situation of your life.

4. Get in touch with any painful event, negative memory, destructive or sinful habits that keep you in bondage. Imagine the healing love of Jesus embracing you now in this area of your life.

5. Invite Jesus to reach back into time and heal the hurt that comes from negative self-concepts, broken relationships, and feelings of turbulence such as unworthiness, guilt, hate, anger, revenge, etc. As you pray, imagine Jesus releasing from within you every thought, word, behavior, image, or feeling that keeps you from loving God and others.

6. Be conscious of any fears you have in your relationship with God. Is there anything that keeps you from the kind of loving relationship you believe God desires with you? Write down any insights, feelings, or images that you become aware of. Or if you want, use music, song, dance, drawing, or other art form to get in

touch with your response to this question. Ask God to heal anything that blocks a more intimate relationship.

7. Pray for any healing needed in family, friends, and community of faith. Pray for the opportunity to be an instrument of Jesus' healing love to your family, friends, and community of faith.

Day Two

Now there was a woman
who had been suffering from hemorrhages for twelve years.
She had endured much under many physicians,
and had spent all that she had;
and she was no better, but rather grew worse.
She had heard about Jesus,
and came up behind him in the crowd and touched his cloak,
for she said, "If I but touch his clothes, I will be made well."
Immediately her hemorrhage stopped;
and she felt in her body that she was healed of her disease.
Immediately aware that power had gone forth from him,
Jesus turned about in the crowd and said,
"Who touched my clothes?"
And his disciples said to him,
"You see the crowd pressing in on you;
how can you say,'Who touched me?'"
He looked all around to see who had done it.
But the woman, knowing what had happened to her,
came in fear and trembling, fell down before him,
and told him the whole truth.
He said to her, "Daughter, your faith has made you well;
go in peace, and be healed of your disease."

Mark 5:25–34

Reflections

1. The risk-taking woman with a hemorrhage reveals woman's dignity as a person. What can this woman teach us in her struggle for wholeness?

2. How is this courageous, assertive woman a model for women today in their struggle to take responsibility for their lives? In their struggles for liberation from patriarchal structures?

3. What is the significance of this story for hierarchy in the church today? What steps can the bishops take to undo the structures that foster male superiority and female inferiority in the church? How can bishops foster the discipleship of equals in the church today?

4. How can women contribute to the liberation of church and society from structures that oppress women? What can women do to give birth to this new model?

Prayer Experiences

1. Be aware of your breathing . . . your breathing in and your breathing out. As you breathe in, breathe in God's healing love. As you breathe out, breathe out peace. As you breathe in, breathe in God's love empowering women. As you breathe out, breathe out God's courage acting in women.

2. Have a sense of God's liberating and healing presence in your life and in the lives of women and men who work for justice and equality in the church and world today.

3. Read the story of the hemorrhaging woman as if you are the woman. After twelve years of attending doctors, you are broke. Everything and everyone you have turned to has disappointed you. You are stigmatized as unclean, cut off from friends and family, physically, emotionally, and spiritually drained. You have heard about Jesus and decide to find him. When you catch a glimpse of him, it is a mob scene. You are afraid of being trampled on. But you know that this time nothing will stop you. You are responsible for your life. You decide to push your way through the crowd to where you can touch Jesus' clothes. Immediately, you feel healing power flowing through your body. The bleeding stops. New energy and a powerful sense of well-being fill you. Jesus turns around and asks who touched him. You become anxious of exposing yourself to the crowd. You are fearful of being once again an object of ridicule. Yet something marvelous has happened. You sense a deep courage to move forward. You look into Jesus' eyes. His words affirm you, a woman with dignity who has been made whole: "Daughter, your faith has made you well; go in peace, and be healed of your disease."

4. As you reflect on the story of this assertive woman, be aware of any feelings, insights, sensations, or images of God's healing love that emerge. Dialogue with this woman about your struggle for wholeness.

5. Reflect on this courageous woman as a role model for women today in their struggle to take responsibility for their lives. Dialogue with her about the struggle women face in their struggle for liberation from patriarchal structures in church and society.

6. Reflect on contemporary women who are prophets in bringing about the reign of God in our time. Create a litany in thanksgiving for all of them. Remember women who work for justice and equality in your own community.

7. Decide on a choice, commitment, or action you can take this week that will further women's dignity, change their status, make use of their gifts, and empower them to take responsibility for their lives.

WEEK THREE
Day Three

Soon afterwards Jesus went to a town called Nain
and his disciples and a large crowd went with him.
As he approached the gate of the town,
a man who had died was being carried out.
He was his mother's only son, and she was a widow;
and with her was a large crowd from the town.
When the Lord saw her, he had compassion for her
and said to her, "Do not weep."
Then he came forward and touched the bier,
and the bearers stood still.
And he said, "Young man, I say to you, rise!"
The dead man sat up and began to speak,
and Jesus gave him to his mother.

Luke 7:11–15

Reflections

Jesus observes the grief of the widow of Nain, has compassion on her, tells her not to weep, and raises up her son.

1. Did you ever grieve over the death of someone you loved? If so, what was this experience like for you? How can Jesus' ministry to the widow of Nain be a source of comfort to those who grieve the death of a loved one?

2. Were you aware of the comforting presence of God during your time of grief? If so, what was that like for you? If not, what may have prevented you from being aware of God's presence?

3. Are there any losses confronting you at the present time?

4. What is God calling you to do to comfort those you know who are mourning a major loss in their lives?

Prayer Experiences

1. Begin your prayer time by finding a quiet place. Become attentive to your body. Wiggle your toes, look at the palm of your hand, listen to your heartbeat, feel your muscles, etc. Be aware of your uniqueness and of God's presence in your body.

2. Get in touch with the strengths and gifts of your physical being. Speak to God about your specialness. Listen to God's response.

3. Following a period of silence, read the scripture passage.

4. Now reread this passage as if you are one of the following: the widow, the son, a member of the crowd, or Jesus. How did you feel as you became a participant in this story? What did you experience when you were the grieving widow? How did it feel to be the deceased son brought back to life by Jesus? What did you experience as a member of the crowd, observing the funeral procession? How did it feel to be Jesus as you encountered the widow and her son? What new insights did you gain into yourself as a result of your meditation?

5. Take time to reflect on how you handle loss and grief in your life. Be aware of any images, feelings, insights, sensations, or memories that emerge. Draw a picture of them or describe them in poetry, song, dance, or in another creative way. Be aware of any feelings, images, sensations, or insights that occur as you do this.

6. Be aware of any unresolved grief issues that emerged in #5. Spend some time sharing your feelings

about them with God. Open yourself to anything God may want to do to comfort you, love you, heal you, strengthen you, or empower you. Imagine God embracing you in your grief with unimaginable tenderness.

7. Pray for all people throughout the world who are mourning the loss of a loved one. Decide on something you can do to comfort someone you know who has suffered a major loss, e.g., death of a family member, divorce, or a serious health problem such as amputation, mastectomy, AIDS.

WEEK THREE
Day Four

Peace I leave with you,
my peace I give to you.
I do not give to you as the world gives.
Do not let your hearts be troubled,
and do not let them be afraid.

John 14:27

Reflections

1. Name one thing that has happened to you recently that caused anxiety. How did you handle it?

2. Do you experience peace in the midst of life's hassles? If so, describe it. If not, why?

3. How can prayer free you from fear?

4. Do you know anyone who is participating in a twelve-step program? If so, ask for an explanation of the steps to serenity. Or call the local chapter of Alcoholics Anonymous, Al Anon, or Overeaters Anonymous and ask for literature on the steps to recovery. When you have done some reflection on the steps, be aware of some ways you can apply them to your life.

Prayer Experiences

1. Sit quietly, comfortable and relaxed. Move to your center by imaging yourself descending a mountain or diving into a deep pool.

2. In the stillness, open yourself to receive the gift of God's peace, shalom, harmony, wholeness. Repeat the word "peace" or "shalom" slowly within yourself in harmony with your breathing. As you do so, image God's healing and hallowing love touching every area of your body, mind, and spirit, freeing you from fear and filling you with peace.

3. Be aware of any fresh images, new insights that emerge from your subconscious. Write these down in your journal.

4. Read this scripture passage slowly, pausing to allow the words and phrases to enter within you. Imagine Jesus speaking the words directly to you. Allow the fullness of Jesus' peace to embrace you.

5. Reflect on the fear and anxiety that your family and friends face. Imagine Jesus speaking these words to each of them. See Jesus embracing each one in his (her) need with healing and peace.

6. According to Jews, shalom, a greeting and farewell that means peace, involves the continual quest for the healing-hallowing elements of our lives. Reflect on the healing-hallowing elements in your life. Ask God to reveal how you can grow in a deeper awareness of your integrity and wholeness.

7. Attend Alcoholics Anonymous, Al Anon, or some other organization that uses the twelve-step approach to recovery. Or ask your the chapter of Alcoholics Anonymous, Al Anon, Overeaters Anonymous for the name and phone number of someone who would be willing to share the program with you. Reflect on their search for peace and serenity. Be aware of anything you can learn from their struggles that will help you in your inner journey toward healing.

Day Five

Now Simon's mother-in-law was in bed with a fever,
and they told Jesus about her at once.
He came and took her by the hand
and lifted her up.
Then the fever left her,
and she began to serve them.

Mark 1:30–31

Reflections

1. The healing of Peter's mother-in-law demonstrates the relationship between healing and service: "The fever left her, and she began to serve them." Recall a particular time when you experienced God's love restoring a family member or friend to physical, emotional, or spiritual health. Did this experience help them to reach out to help others? If so, describe the event. What difference did it make for you to discover God touching someone you love?

2. Why is it important for families and communities to pray together for healing for one another?

3. Can you identify an area in you that needs healing? Would you be willing to ask family, friends, members of the Christian community to pray with you for healing?

4. What does it mean to be a "wounded healer," one who is aware of his (her) own brokenness and wounds and in spite of this reaches out in love to serve others who have similar problems? How can families, neighbors, communities do this? Have you ever been a "wounded healer" for someone else? Give specific examples from your experience.

Prayer Experiences

1. Quiet yourself; be still inside and out. Relax. Breathe in deeply and breathe out deeply for several minutes.

2. Read Mark 1:30–31. Enter the story as if you are there. Observe what happens; listen to what is being said. Become part of this healing encounter with Jesus. Assume the role of Peter's mother-in-law. Be aware of what she experiences as a person with a fever, as Jesus takes her by the hand and lifts her up, as she is healed, as she shows her gratitude by serving Jesus and his disciples. Dialogue with Peter's mother-in-law about this extraordinary meeting with Jesus. Listen as Jesus shares his feelings, insights, and memories of this vibrant woman.

3. Compose a litany of thanksgiving for all the times God has restored you, family members, or friends to physical, emotional, or spiritual health. Record this litany in your prayer journal so that you can offer thanks often for God's healing in your life.

4. Ask a member of your family or community to pray with you for healing for yourself or someone you love. For example, husbands and wives could pray for healing in their marriage. A mother and father could pray with their children for release from stress and anxiety, healing of low self-esteem, healing of a bad cold, healing from hostility, etc.

5. Some examples of "wounded healers": People who minister effectively out of a sense of their wounds or struggles are recovering drug addicts who minister

powerfully to drug addicts; survivors of breast cancer who encourage women who have just been diagnosed with this disease; people suffering grief or tragedy in their lives who join support groups to find strength from others who are coping with similar loss. Spend some time praying for all such "wounded healers" who lovingly share God's healing love with others.

6. Become aware of any way God is calling you to be a "wounded healer." Ask God to reveal how you can share with others your experience of God's healing love in the midst of your sinfulness, brokenness, and woundedness.

7. Image Jesus looking directly into your eyes. Hear him say, "(your name), in my wounds, your (name your woundedness, brokenness, sinfulness) has been healed." Repeat these words as a mantra slowly and prayerfully as long as you want. As you pray, imagine Jesus touching, embracing, lifting you up, doing whatever needs to be done to make you whole and holy, so that you can serve others with compassion.

Day Six

In the beginning all creatures were green and vital;
they flourished amidst flowers.
Later the green figure itself came down.[10]

O life-giving greenness of God's hand,
with which he has planted an orchard.
You rise resplendent into the highest heavens,
like a towering pillar.
You are glorious in God's work.
And you, O mountain heights,
will never waver when God tests you.
Although you stand in the distance as if in exile,
No armed power is mighty enough to attack you.
You are glorious in God's work.[11]

Hildegard of Bingen

Reflections

1. Hildegard of Bingen celebrates the greening power of creation and humanity. For her, healing is the return of greening power and moisture. "The soul is the freshness of the flesh, for the body grows and thrives through it just as Earth becomes fruitful through moisture."[12]
How would you describe the environmental degradation of Earth today?

2. How can we individually and collectively take responsibility for the harm done to Earth?

3. In what ways can Earth become our guide in showing us how to be healers in touch with the needs of the planet?

4. Why is it important to work for structural and systemic change in environmental practices and polices in our society?

Prayer Experiences

1. Find a comfortable and restful position. Close your eyes. Imagine the air that surrounds you is like an immense ocean, filled with God's healing energy and power. You are drawing in God's healing energy every time you breathe in. As you breathe in, fill your lungs with divine energy. As you breathe out, imagine you are breathing out all negative feelings, your anxieties, your impurities. Image your whole body becoming a radiant reflection of God's healing love by breathing in God's healing power and breathing out all negativity.

2. Now as you breathe in and out slowly and deeply, imagine Earth breathing in healing energy and breathing out toxic waste, contamination of the air, all types of pollution, etc. Imagine you see the whole planet becoming radiant and alive by breathing in God's hallowing energy and "greening power" and breathing out all impurities.

3. Go outside and contemplate Earth. Explore the grass and clay underneath with both your hands. Feel its texture, its smoothness or roughness, its softness or hardness, its coldness or warmth. Look at its colors, its form, its layers. Invite Earth to be your guide in helping you to understand the profound mystery of its existence. Ask Earth questions about its life, its origins, its future. Listen while Earth reveals its mysteries to you. Ask Earth what it needs from you for healing, harmony, and wholeness. Open yourself to receive healing from the planet.

4. Reflect on what you can do individually and collectively to take responsibility for the harm done to

Earth. Think about ways you can maintain quality of life but decrease consumption of energy or materials. For example, reducing consumption of red meat could result in giving back millions of acres of U.S. meat-production land to prairies and woodlands. Cutting down on red meats and fats in our diets also results in improved health.

5. Invite Mother Earth to preach a "sermon" about healing Earth. Listen to and share with others what she reveals. Be aware of the challenges this sermon might have on our present social structures.

6. Develop an attitude of reverence for all inanimate creation. St. Francis of Assisi treated the sun and moon, the stars and trees as family members he talked to and deeply cherished. Go outside and talk, sing, dance, laugh, celebrate with all living things the beauty of God's creation.

7. Decide on actions, choices, or commitments you will make to join with others in working for changes in environmental policies and practices. Some possiblities: boycotting companies with poor environmental practices; joining or supporting organizations that lobby for legislation that will protect the environment; reporting to the proper authorities and to the media those companies, businesses, agencies whose policies or practices damage Earth.

Day Seven

According to Meister Eckhart,
compassion is the name for Yahweh
and Yahweh's presence with us.
Compassion bestows heavenly blessings on us
and initiates the end time which is the time
of our final healing and salvation and of full happiness.
Compassion is the first and ultimate blessing
we receive and give.
"People who have let go of themselves are so pure
that the world cannot harm them . . .
People who love justice will be admitted to justice.
They will be seized by justice, and will be one with justice.
When we encounter God
we encounter justice and compassion. . . ."[13]

In Eckhart's words,
"The first of God's works is compassion . . .
and the highest work of God is . . . compassion."
Compassion means doing for others.
We are to give birth to compassion by doing justice
and relieving the sufferings of others.
Eckhart supports his view
by quoting chapter 58 of Isaiah in his sermon:
"Is not this the sort of fast that pleases me . . .
to break unjust fetters and undo the thongs of the yoke,
to let the oppressed go free, and break every yoke,
to share your bread with the hungry,
and shelter the homeless poor. . . ."[14]

Reflections

Meister Eckhart believed that the heart of the spiritual journey is compassion. For him, compassion means healing interwoven with justice. According to him, "Your entire life will be called healed when you have entered into compassion and its works of justice."

1. Reflect on the world today. Where do you see oppression, discrimination, and injustice?

2. In what ways are we called to respond to these issues with courage and strength? How are you presently involved in helping others experience liberation and healing in their lives?

3. How do you see God healing and transforming the world today through people, groups, and organizations dedicated to justice and compassion?

4. As a result of your reflection on God's healing love for all humanity and for the entire cosmos, what do you feel called to do?

Prayer Experiences

1. Begin by quieting yourself in the presence of God. Light a candle if you wish, or play soft meditative music. Breathe deeply. Simply relax for a few minutes.

2. Read Meister Eckhart's insights slowly and allow a word, phrase, or image to touch you.

3. If a word or phrase comes to mind, you may wish to repeat it as a mantra or prayer phrase. As you do so, imagine yourself living as a person of justice and compassion in your daily relationships and activities.

4. Pray for all people in the world today who suffer from oppression, discrimination, and injustice. Pray for all women and men who work for justice and compassion in our world.

5. Be aware of any images, words, feelings, or insights that describe your experience of God as challenger of unjust structures and liberator of those who suffer oppression today.

6. Compassion, according to Eckhart, initiates the end time, which is the time of our final healing and salvation and of full blessing. Image this breaking forth of compassion in our world. All people treat one another and all creation with respect and love. The entire cosmos experiences the explosion of grace, goodness, creativity, justice, tenderness, happiness, and joy. Imagine yourself living in the fullness of God's love and glory with all humanity and the entire cosmos. What thoughts, feelings, images, sensations emerge?

7. Reflect on ways you can help others to experience justice and healing in their lives. Decide on one thing you will do to make this happen. Some examples are: serving at a soup kitchen or homeless shelter, volunteering to work with groups or agencies that respond to victims of abuse, crime, discrimination, etc.

W<small>EEK</small> F<small>OUR</small>

Living Our Empowerment

An important issue today is how to live the spiritual life. One of the great truths I discovered is that spirituality involves opening oneself to the empowerment of the Spirit in the ordinary events of life. God's radiance shines from the face of my 81-year-old mother as she sits for hours in another world, quietly fingering her rosary beads, absorbed in prayer. As our family struggles to cope with the sickness and diminishment that she is facing, we feel God's presence strengthening us. God is very near. We don't take each other for granted as much any more. Every day is a precious gift. As we sit around with our afternoon tea, listening, laughing, interrupting, encouraging, advising, and supporting one another, we realize how blessed we are simply to be together as a family. Playing games with Katie, my three-year-old niece and with Danny, my twenty-month-old nephew renews my "inner child" and helps me to delight in the small miracles of flowers and bugs, stars and sunshine, balls and dolls.

Using feminine images of God as a resource for prayer, as I speak to groups around the world, gives me a sense that a fuller imaging of God and a developing feminine consciousness are part of a fundamental shift in thinking today. The universal models, or images, that have for centuries supported our life-view concerning the meaning of life—our relationships with others and with God—are no longer able to support the new evolving situations. As old models crumble, new ones are gradually replacing them. The old models are not supporting the world and cosmic consciousness that is barreling in on us, and the new ones are not yet fully in place. We stand between what is passing and what is not yet totally visible. What we need, those of us who live in this inch of time "between," is an empowerment that will enable us to minister as transitional leaders, as bridges from yesterday to tomorrow for those who need safe passage.

The Spirit of Jesus is that empowerment. "But you will receive power when the Holy Spirit has come upon you; and you will be my witnesses in Jerusalem, in all Judea and Samaria, and to the ends of Earth." Christians throughout the ages have experienced the empowerment of the Spirit in their lives. The apostles, some women disciples, and Mary the mother of Jesus were present in the Upper Room on Pentecost when the Holy Spirit appeared in the form of tongues of fire. All were empowered to proclaim the good news of salvation. Today Christians are experiencing this same empowerment in their lives. They are discovering a variety of ways to be witnesses to the Spirit in their families, communities, churches, neighborhoods, and the world.

In the twentieth century, Edith Stein and Thomas Merton, outstanding people of faith and wisdom whose spiritual lives have inspired millions, demonstrate the empowerment of the Spirit in our age.

Edith Stein was born and raised in a Jewish family in Germany. In 1922, she converted to Catholicism and later became a Carmelite nun. Refusing to deny her Jewish heritage and proclaiming her solidarity with the Jewish people, she was arrested by the Nazis and put to death at Auschwitz on August 9, 1942. As a mystic, a prominent philosopher, and a woman of heroic courage, Edith Stein speaks powerfully to us today of a hope that transcends suffering and as a witness "to the profoundest values of human existence, the significance of the individual, and the truths of faith that can reconcile Christian and Jew, philosophy and religion, oppressor and oppressed to heal a troubled world."[15] Stein demonstrates through her life and writings that living our empowerment requires a consciousness of God's presence in all aspects of life, especially in times of darkness and suffering:

> Who are you, kindly light, who fill me now,
> And brighten all the darkness of my heart?
> You guide me forward like a mother's hand,
> And if you let me go, I could not take a single step
> alone.

Thomas Merton was a Cistercian monk, a contemplative and prophetic figure whose reverence for the ordinary blessings of life and insights into the heart of the human person have made a profound contribution to the spirituality of our day. A love for solitude and the natural world are recurring themes in Merton's works. His writings are filled with wisdom for those striving to live their empowerment as Christians. According to Merton, the darkness of faith shines most brightly in the light of wisdom. "Hagia Sophia in all things is the Divine Life reflected in . . . all things like the air receiving the sunlight. She is life as communion, life as thanksgiving, life as praise, life as festival, life as glory."[16]

Merton uses the metaphor or image of the cosmic dance to describe the meaning of living in the contemporary world:

> When we are alone on a starlit night, when by
> chance we see the migrating birds in autumn descending on a grove of junipers to rest and eat;
> when we see children in a moment when they are
> really children, when we know love in our own
> hearts . . . all these provide a glimpse of the cosmic
> dance.[17]

The reflections in Week Four invite us to live our empowerment in the midst of the hectic, stress-filled challenges of life today. The Spirit empowers us with the all we need to live the Christian life fully. Drawing a stark contrast between "life according to the flesh" and "life in the Spirit," St. Paul challenges us to examine the areas or aspects of our lives that need to change before we can live a fuller "life in the Spirit." Through the Holy Spirit, we have been called and gifted for ministry in the community. By our baptisms we have been empowered by the Spirit to love and minister to others. It is important to reflect on the specific ways we can use our gifts to make a difference in people's lives.

Living our empowerment in the world means serving the needs of the poor and the oppressed throughout the world. When we do this, we learn that in order to be effective agents of change we need to understand the causes of poverty and oppression. This means analyzing and critiquing the social structures that cause people to suffer from lack of food, adequate housing, violence, etc. Statistics demonstrate that one-third of the world is over-consuming the world's natural resources and squandering the resources of future generations.

One of the ways we can make a difference is to join with others to lobby for human rights, justice, environmental policies that protect the land, provide food and shelter for the poor and oppressed, etc. As Christians committed to living the gospel, it is our role to challenge corporations, governments, and institutions to create socially responsible policies that promote the well-being of all people, not just the vested interests of the rich and powerful. Then we will be able to stand with the righteous in Matthew's gospel (25:37–40) and hear God say: "Truly I tell you, just as you did it to one of the least of these who are members of my family, you did it to me."

In the hectic, stress-filled pace of contemporary life, discover the Spirit empowering you for loving service to others. Embrace your Divine Partner in the cosmic dance of life. Invite the Spirit of God to minister to you and through you to family, friends, neighbors, community members, the church, the poor, the oppressed, the suffering of the world. Open yourself to living your empowerment in the following prayer reflections.

WEEK FOUR
Day One

Jesus said: "But you will receive power
when the Holy Spirit has come upon you;
and you will be my witnesses in Jerusalem,
in all Judea and Samaria, and to the ends of Earth."

Acts 1:8

When the day of Pentecost had come,
they were all together in one place.
And suddenly from heaven there came a sound
like the rush of a violent wind,
and it filled the entire house where they were sitting.
Divided tongues, as of fire, appeared among them,
and a tongue rested on each of them.
All of them were filled with the Holy Spirit
and began to speak in other languages,
as the Spirit gave them ability.

Acts 2:1–4

Reflections

1. What does it mean for Christians to be empowered by the Spirit today?

2. Reflect on your faith journey. Where have you been? Where are you going? Recall a time when you became especially aware of the Spirit's presence in your life. How did your life change as a result of these experiences?

3. What can you do to be more open to the Spirit?

4. In what ways can you be a witness of the Spirit in your family, community, church, neighborhood, and the world?

Prayer Experiences

1. Breathe deeply. While you breathe in, be aware of God's Spirit filling your lungs with divine energy. While you breathe out, imagine you are breathing out God's life-giving Spirit to the whole world.

2. Pray for the Spirit to fill the hearts of your family, friends, community, and all people with this prayer:

> *Come, Holy Spirit, fill the hearts of your faithful*
> *and kindle in them the fire of your love.*
> *Send forth your Spirit, O Lord,*
> *and renew the face of Earth.*

3. Draw a road to symbolize your life. Begin with birth and conclude with this year. Write down the important events and experiences on your faith journey. As you do so, be aware of any thoughts, feelings, images, sensations, and memories that emerge.

4. Recall a time when you became especially aware of the Spirit's presence in your life. Draw a mandala or an image of your experience of the Spirit's presence in your life at that time.

5. Read the story of Pentecost (Acts 2:1–4). Imagine that you are present. Imagine the Holy Spirit coming down on you: "Divided tongues, as of fire, appeared among them, and a tongue rested on each of them. All of them were filled with the Holy Spirit . . . " See yourself filled with the Holy Spirit . . . leaving the room . . . returning to your home . . . family . . . friends . . . job . . . neighborhood . . . community . . . church . . . world. You are aware that the Spirit is living in you, loving through

you, working through you in every aspect of your life.

6. Remember people who have been witnesses of the presence of the Spirit for you. Write a thank you note to one of them.

7. Remember people for whom you have been a witness of the presence of the Spirit. Pray for them. Be aware of ways you can be a witness of the Spirit's presence in your family, community, church, neighborhood, and the world.

Day Two

Live by the Spirit, I say,
and do not gratify the desires of the flesh.
For what the flesh desires is opposed to the Spirit,
and what the Spirit desires is opposed to the flesh;
for these are opposed to each other,
to prevent you from doing what you want.
But if you are led by the Spirit,
you are not subject to the law.
Now the works of the flesh are obvious:
fornication, impurity, licentiousness, idolatry, sorcery,
enmities, strife, jealousy, anger, quarrels,
dissensions, factions, envy, drunkenness, carousing,
and things like these.
I am warning you, as I warned you before:
those who do such things
will not inherit the kingdom of God.
By contrast, the fruit of the Spirit is love, joy, peace,
patience, kindness, generosity, faithfulness,
gentleness and self-control.
There is no law against such things.
If we live by the Spirit,
let us also be guided by the Spirit.
Let us not become conceited,
competing against one another, envying one another.

Galatians 5:16–23, 25–26

Reflections

1. St. Paul shows a stark contrast between "life according to the flesh" and "life in the Spirit" in this passage. How are people today living "according to the flesh"? How are people living "life in the Spirit"?

2. In what ways are you living "according to the flesh"? In what ways are you living "life in the Spirit"?

3. What areas or aspects do you need to change in order to experience a fuller "life in the Spirit"?

4. What fruits of the Spirit do you see in your life? How can you share these fruits with others?

Prayer Experiences

1. Feel your breath . . . Breathe in and out slowly. As you breathe, open yourself to the presence of the Spirit filling you with love . . . joy . . . peace . . . patience . . . kindness . . . generosity . . . faithfulness . . . gentleness . . . self-control.

2. Image the Spirit dancing within you . . . leaping . . . stepping . . . twirling . . . gliding . . . tapping . . . skipping . . . moving to the melodious rhythms of the music of life within you.

3. Become aware of the different "steps" the Spirit has taught you. Get in touch with the "movements" of the Spirit within you. List the fruits that you have discovered in your dance with your divine partner. Offer thanks for them.

4. Reflect on changes you need to make in order to be able to dance more gracefully with your divine partner. Ask the Spirit to choreograph a life-transforming dance for you. For example, "Come, Holy Spirit; leap with joy in me in times of sadness and loneliness. Come, Holy Spirit; step with me through my fears and anxieties, embrace me with your perfect peace."

5. Imagine the disciples who were present at Pentecost dancing with the Spirit of God in the early days of the church. Observe the courage, enthusiasm, strength, faith, and love of Mary of Nazareth, Peter, Mary of Magdala, John, Paul, Priscilla, Lydia, Timothy, and others.

6. Imagine that the reign of God has come. See all hu-

manity, all creation, all the saints and angels, your family, friends, members of your community, and yourself joining together in the "Cosmic Dance of the Spirit." As you do so, be aware of any thoughts, feelings, images, sensations that emerge.

7. Put on some feet-tapping music and dance your hopes and dreams of living a fuller "life in the Spirit" now.

WEEK FOUR
Day Three

Now there are varieties of gifts, but the same Spirit;
and there are varieties of services, but the same Lord;
and there are varieties of activities, but it is the same God
who activates all of them in everyone.
To each is given the manifestation of the Spirit
for the common good.
To one is given through the Spirit
the utterance of wisdom,
and to another the utterance of knowledge
according to the same Spirit,
to another faith by the same Spirit,
to another gifts of healing by the one Spirit,
to another the working of miracles, to another prophecy,
to another the discernment of spirits,
to another various kinds of tongues,
to another the interpretation of tongues.
All these are activated by one and the same Spirit,
who allots to each one individually just as the Spirit chooses.

1 Corinthians 12:4–11

Reflections

1. Through the Holy Spirit, we have been called and gifted for ministry in the community. By our baptisms we have been empowered by the Spirit to love and minister to others. What gifts has the Spirit given you for ministry? Be as specific as you can in identifying them.

2. What do you see as your ministry now?

3. Who are powerful witnesses to the gospel in our time?

4. In what ways have you used your gifts to make a difference in people's lives?

Prayer Experiences

1. Play some of your favorite, mellow, classical music. Do some stretching exercises. Relax your mind, body, spirit. Be aware that you (with all your gifts and flaws) reflect God's glory. You are an image of God. When people see you, they see God's presence in our world. To remind you of this, repeat one of the following affirmations throughout the day: "I reflect God's glory." "I am a radiant image of God's love to the world." "My body is God's dwelling place."

2. Read the scripture passage. Allow the words, phrases, and sentences to sink deeply into your consciousness. Reflect on Christian communities where you have experienced the gifts of the Spirit working for the common good. Offer thanks for these communities.

3. As you look back on your life, reflect on how you have used your gifts to help others. One way to do this is to recall how you have used each of your senses to make a difference in people's lives. For example: With my hands I baked bread, held my baby, dried a friend's tears, etc. With my voice I comforted a neighbor in her loss, I called a lonely person, I spoke up for equality at work. With my feet I stood in line a long time in the grocery store to buy food for my family; I walked, jumped, played for hours with my children. With my ears I listened to endless complaints about my parents' health, etc.

4. After identifying your gifts, draw a mandala. Fill it with the different ways you use the Spirit's gifts to minister to others. Offer thanks for your gifts and ministry.

5. Be aware of people you have known or heard about who are powerful witnesses to the gospel in our time. What have they been willing to risk? How do they use the gifts of the Spirit to change the world? Write a dialogue with one of them.

6. Pray for the Spirit to guide you in your ministry. Ask the Spirit to help you find new ways to be "good news" for others.

7. Write a prayer of dedication to your ministry. Place it in a prominent place and pray it often. If you want, share or pray it with those to whom you minister.

WEEK FOUR
Day Four

God is a stronghold for the oppressed,
a stronghold in times of trouble.
And those who know your name
put their trust in you,
for you, O God, have not forsaken those who seek you.

For the needy shall not always be forgotten,
nor the hope of the poor perish forever.

Psalm 9:10–11,19

Reflections

1. Consider the needs of the poor and oppressed throughout the world. What injustices cause famine, hunger, homelessness, violence in our time?

2. As you think about the suffering of the afflicted and poor across the globe, where do you see God being revealed in it?

3. Why is it important to analyze the social structures that cause people to suffer from lack of food, adequate housing, violence, etc.?

4. From statistics we know that one-third of the world is over-consuming Earth's natural resources and squandering the resources of future generations. In what ways can you join with others to lobby for human rights, justice, environmental policies that protect Earth, food, and shelter for the poor and oppressed? Why is it important to challenge corporations, governments, and institutions to create socially responsible policies that promote the well-being of all people, and not just the vested interest of the rich and powerful?

Prayer Experiences

1. Make yourself comfortable, close your eyes, and begin to let yourself relax. Simply become aware of your breath moving in and moving out. Continue doing this for several minutes.

2. As you read Psalm 9, reflect on the needs of the poor people of the world. Be aware of the injustices that cause their suffering and deprivation.

3. Become aware of God's presence. Imagine God delivering the poor and oppressed from poverty, hate, abuse, hunger, homelessness, and violence. See them experiencing freedom, justice, peace, equality, and love. All are empowered by God, the stronghold of the oppressed, to live life to the full. Be aware of the connectedness of God's people with creation.

4. Compose a psalm, song, or poem expressing your vision and hope for empowerment of the poor and oppressed people.

5. Conduct an examination of conscience on your use of food, clothing, electricity, water, oil, gas, and other resources. Be aware of ways you can save and share more of your time, energy, money, food, clothing, and resources with the poor and needy.

6. Create a social examination of conscience for one institution you are familiar with, such as church, school, or your place of work. Examine how their policies, procedures, programs promote social awareness and responsibility in any of the following areas: human rights, poverty, hunger, homelessness, environmental healing, peace, and justice.

7. Get politically involved. Become an activist for the poor and needy in your own neighborhood, community, state. Do what you can. A few possibilities are: write letters; raise consciousness; share with friends; join action groups that work for change; lobby for laws, programs, and policies that will create jobs for the unemployed, low-cost housing for the poor, school lunch programs, free health care for the needy, emergency housing for the homeless, meals for the hungry, crime- and drug-free communities; join a neighborhood crime watch, a consumer advocate group.

WEEK FOUR
Day Five

Then these just will ask,
"When did we see you hungry and feed you,
or see you thirsty and give you drink?
When did we see you as a stranger and invite you in,
or clothe you in your nakedness?
When did we see you ill or in prison
and come to visit you?"
The ruler will answer them,
"I assure you,
every time you did it for the least of my sisters or brothers,
you did it for me."[18]

Matthew 25:37–40

Reflections

1. As you look around the world, where do you see people in need of the basic necessities?

2. In what ways are those you know suffering physical, emotional, or spiritual hunger? Loneliness? Sickness? Isolation? Homelessness?

3. Why is it important to avoid burnout in your ministry to others? What can we do to avoid burnout and stress?

4. Is there anything you feel called to do to minister to your own needs? To the needs of others?

Prayer Experiencess

1. Choose a quiet place to rest and spend some time being attentive to something of beauty around you. Or see yourself in a place of natural beauty, somewhere on a high mountain, near the ocean, by a quiet stream, in a meadow, etc. Notice the colors, shapes, odors, textures, and sounds. Be aware of God's presence with you and in you.

2. Read the newspaper daily. Be conscious of the sufferings of people throughout the world. As you read, see each person you read about as Christ. Pray for each situation, as you feel moved by compassion to do so.

3. Read Matthew 25:37–40. Reflect on the ways that you provide nourishment, shelter, clothing, security, comfort, forgiveness, care for your family, friends, neighbors, or strangers. Offer thanks for the times that you have loved and served them as if they were Christ. Ask God for forgiveness for your failures to love them in this way.

4. Be attentive to family, friends, neighbors, community, church members, or strangers who are experiencing any of the following: physical hunger, spiritual hunger, loneliness, sickness, isolation, or homelessness. Ask God for the gift of a compassionate heart and for an opportunity to serve someone who needs the love of Christ. Decide on one act of service you will do for at least one person in the coming week.

5. Be aware of the dangers of burnout in your life. Ask God to help you forgive yourself for the times you have failed to love and serve the Christ within you, for the

times you neglected your own health and emotional needs, for the times you treated yourself harshly, for the times you pushed yourself too hard to achieve unrealistic goals, for the times you acted as if you were superhuman in your service of others, etc.

6. Take some time to be attentive to your own needs. Get in touch with your body—any tightness, pain, aches, stress you may be feeling. Listen to your emotions—any anger, fear, worry, anger, or hurt you may be carrying. Reflect on your relationship with God and others, your spiritual life, your prayer, your attitude to family, friends, and co-workers. Be aware of how much time you allow for rest and relaxation. Invite Christ to minister to your deepest needs. Imagine Christ renewing, refreshing, revitalizing, empowering you.

Now imagine people who are hungry and thirsty for physical or spiritual nourishment; people who are sick physically, emotionally, or spiritually; the homeless, lonely, depressed; those imprisoned by prejudice, hostility, or addiction. See yourself either alone or with others responding to their needs in whatever way you can. Be aware of all the ways you have been, are, and will be a living embodiment of Christ's compassion to those who suffer in your family, community, neighborhood, church, and world. See Christ smile at you, and say: "(your name), just as you did it to one of the least of these who are members of my family, you did it to me."

7. Draw a mandala or image of one or two ways you plan to minister to the Christ within you and to the Christ within others. Put this mandala or image in a prominent area as a reminder of your commitment to live as an empowered disciple of Christ.

Day Six

Who are you, kindly light, who fill me now,
And brighten all the darkness of my heart?
You guide me forward like a mother's hand,
And if you let me go,
I could not take a single step alone.
You are the space,
Embracing all my being, hidden in it.
Loosened from you, I fall in the abyss
Of nothingness, from which you draw my life.
Nearer to me than I myself am,
And more within me than my inmost self,
You are outside my grasp, beyond my reach,
And what name can contain you?
You, Holy Spirit, you, eternal Love![19]

Edith Stein

Reflections

1. Journeying to wholeness and holiness requires a consciousness of God's presence in all aspects of life, especially in times of darkness and suffering. How does Edith Stein's insights reflect this awareness?

2. Sometimes, as the old saying goes, "we can't see the forest for the trees." This happens when people, for instance, allow one failure or setback to depress them so completely that they see themselves as failures. How does recognizing God's presence help us trust God when things go wrong in our lives?

3. How does an awareness of God's presence affect faith?

4. How is faith related to justice? In what ways can you, like Edith Stein, be a witness for justice to the oppressed and the oppressor?

Prayer Experiences

1. Put on soft instrumental music. Close your eyes. Get in a comfortable position. Imagine that you are in a beautiful place: the seashore with the sound of the waves crashing against the sand, a sparkling, flowing stream or river, a lake surrounded by beautiful trees and wildlife, a peaceful mountain.

2. Imagine the place as clearly as possible . . . See all the colors and shapes . . . Hear all the sounds . . . Speak to the beauty that surrounds you . . . Touch creation with gentle hands . . . Simply "be" in your beautiful place.

3. Now be aware of God's presence in your life past and present during happy times . . . sad times . . . times of anguish . . . times of great suffering and struggle . . . times of bondage . . . times of great liberation . . .

4. Invite God to speak to you now about those memories and how they are part of the divine plan for your life. Listen as God reveals God's hopes and dreams for you . . . promises comfort and strength in your sufferings and struggles . . . affirms your dignity and giftedness . . . expresses infinite love for you . . . empowers you with courage and hope for the future.

5. Be aware of any feelings, images, insights, sensations that emerge. Write down, draw, or express in some creative way such as song, dance, art, music, poetry, anything God has revealed to you that helps you become more aware of God's presence in your life. Ask God to deepen your faith so that no matter what happens you will be ready to say yes to God.

6. Imagine God acting powerfully to break down barriers that keep people enslaved by fear, prejudice, hatred, violence, war, racism, classism, sexism, ageism, etc. Imagine all people living together as one family . . . aware of their human dignity and connectedness . . . living in peace and justice . . . sharing the world's goods and resources . . . working together for the healing of Earth and the common good of humankind . . .

7. Ask God to help you, like Edith Stein, to be a witness for justice to both the oppressed and the oppressors. Decide on one way you will do this in the coming month.

Day Seven

When we are alone on a starlit night,
when by chance we see the migrating birds in autumn
descending on a grove of junipers to rest and eat;
when we see children in a moment
when they are really children,
when we know love in our own hearts;
or when, like the Japanese poet, Basho,
we hear an old frog land in a quiet pond
with a solitary splash—at such times the awakening,
the turning inside out of all values, the "newness,"
the emptiness and the purity of vision
that make themselves evident,
all these provide a glimpse of the cosmic dance.

. . . For the world and time
are the dance of the Lord in emptiness.
The silence of the spheres is the music of a wedding feast.
The more we persist in misunderstanding
the phenomena of life, the more we analyze them
out into strange finalities and complex purposes of our own,
the more we involve ourselves
in sadness, absurdity, and despair.
But it does not matter much,
because no despair of ours can alter the reality of things,
or stain the joy of the cosmic dance which is always there.
Indeed, we are in the midst of it . . .
for it beats in our very blood,
whether we want it to or not.[20]

Thomas Merton

Reflections

Thomas Merton's writings are filled with wisdom for people striving to live the spiritual life today. Among his books that are considered spiritual classics are: *The Sign of Jonas* (1953), *New Seeds of Contemplation* (1962), and *Conjectures of a Guilty Bystander* (1966).

1. What image(s) does Thomas Merton use to describe the spiritual life?

2. Consider how you and all of creation participate in the cosmic dance. Describe what this image means to you.

3. What image(s) would you use to describe how you serve others?

4. What difference does it make to be empowered by the Spirit for ministry? What difference has this made in your ministry?

Prayer Experiences

1. Lie down, or sit down, and take several minutes to get comfortable. Take a few deep breaths to unwind. Relax your face, your shoulders, your limbs, your stomach, your breathing.

2. Be still and listen to your body. Accept yourself as you are at this moment. Whenever tension occurs, whenever anxieties distract you, simply be aware of them and gently let them go. Listen to your breathing. Be aware of your heartbeat. Let each moment, as it comes, be new and fresh. Open yourself to the Spirit present in your whole being.

3. Invite the Spirit to embrace you in the cosmic dance. See yourself twirling, leaping, spinning, tapping, swaying, gliding, being swept off your feet by the Spirit as together you dance through the days and nights of your existence with reckless abandon in love with life . . . in love with your family . . . in love with your friends and relatives . . . in love with your community . . . in love with people . . . in love with creation . . . in love with God.

4. Be aware of any images, feelings, or thoughts that emerge during your cosmic dance. Record these, if you wish, in a journal, in art, poetry, dance, song, or in another creative way.

5. Open yourself to the Spirit's empowerment in your life:
   Come, Spirit, as healing and love.
   Come, Spirit, as nurturing and tenderness.
   Come, Spirit, as wisdom and discernment.

Come, Spirit, as strength and courage.
Come, Spirit, as joy and peace.
etc.

6. Listen as the Spirit empowers you to serve others:
Be a channel of healing love to others.
Nourish people with tender compassion.
Guide others wisely and carefully.
Speak out for the oppressed.
Serve the poor and broken-hearted. Encourage those who have lost hope.
Work for justice.
Serve people with a generous heart.
etc.

7. Reflect on the image that best describes your desire to serve others. Draw or make a symbol of this image. Put this symbol somewhere as a reminder of your call to ministry. Each time you look at this symbol, let it remind you of your commitment to live your empowerment in loving service to others.

Footnotes

Week One
Day One
1. Sue Woodruff, *Meditations With Mechtild of Magdeburg* (Santa Fe: N. M.: Bear & Company, 1982), pp. 34-35.
2. Teresa of Avila, *Soliloquies* quoted in Noteworthy St Teresa of Avila, Terre Haute, Ind.: Carmel of St. Joseph. This quotation is from *The Collected Works of St. Teresa of Avila* by Kieran Kavanaugh, O.C.D. and Otilio Rodriquez, O.C.D., Institute of Carmelite Studies, Washington D.C. 20002.

Day Six
3. *Meditations With Mechtild of Magdeburg*, pp. 34-35.

Day Seven
4. Teresa of Avila, *Soliloquies*.

Week Two
Introduction
5. *The Complete Poems of Thomas Merton* (New York: New Directions, 1977), p. 366.
6. Notre Dame: Ind.: Ave Maria Press, 1992, p. 63.

Day Six
7. Edmund Colledge and James Walsh, *Julian of Norwich: Showings* (New York: Paulist Press, 1978), p. 340.

Week Three
Introduction
8. Aldegundis Fuhrkotter, *Hildegard von Bingen, Brief-wechsel*, transl. Ron Miller (Salzburg, 1965), p. 111.
9. Meister Eckhart, Sermons 30, 31 quoted in Matthew Fox, *Breakthrough: Meister Eckhart's Creation Spirituality in New Translation* (New York: Doubleday, 1980), pp. 431-432, 434.

Day Six
10. The green figure refers to Jesus in the writings of Hildegard of Bingen. Hildegard of Bingen, *Ordo Virtutum Sequentia Ensemble für*

Musik des Mittelaters, WCR Producer (Cologne: EMI Electrola, 1982).

11. Hildegard of Bingen, "In Honor of St. Disibode." This poem appears in Pudentiana Barth, et al., *Hildegard von Bingen: Lieder* (Salzburg, 1969) quoted in *Illuminations of Hildegard of Bingen,* with commentary by Matthew Fox (Santa Fe, N. M.: Bear & Company, 1985), p. 32.

12. Aldegundis Fuhrkotter, *Hildegard von Bingen, Brief-wechsel,* p.111.

Day Seven

13. Meister Eckhart, *Deutsche Predigten und traktate,* ed. and tr. into modern German by Josef Quint (Munich, 1963).

14. Meister Eckhart, Sermons 30, 31 quoted in *Breakthrough: Meister Eckhart's Creation Spirituality in New Translation.*

Week Four
Introduction

15. Waltraud Herbstrith (transl. Bernard Bonowitz, O.S.C.O.), *Edith Stein: A Biography* (San Francisco: Herper & Row, 1985) (book jacket).

16. Thomas Merton, "Emblems for a Season of Fury" in Thomas McDonnell, *Through the Year with Thomas Merton* (New York: Doubleday, 1985), p. 223.

17. Thomas Merton, *New Seeds of Contemplation,* cited in *Through the Year with Thomas Merton,* pp.199-200.

Day Five

18. Year A, *Inclusive Lectionary Texts, A Project of Priests for Equality,* P.O. Box 5243, West Hyattsville, MD 20782, p. 175.

Week Six

19. Edith Stein, *Gedichte und Gebete aus dem Nachlass,* 2d ed., ed. W. Herbstrith (Munich: Verlag G. Kaffke, 1981), pp. 23-24 cited in Waltraud Herbstrith, *Edith Stein: A Biography,* 1985), p. 91.

Day Seven

20. Thomas Merton, *New Seeds of Contemplation,* cited in Thomas McDonnell, *Through the Year with Thomas Merton,* pp. 199-200.

Of Related Interest...

Scripture Reflections Day by Day
Rev. Joseph G. Donders
These 365 Gospel meditations are current, timely, short enough to
be read in any spare moment and full of meaning and hope.

ISBN: 0-89622-494-5, 366 pp, $9.95

Quiet Places with Jesus
Isaias Powers, CP
These 40 meditations begin with Scripture quotations, followed by
reflections and step-by-step methods to meditation.

ISBN: 0-89622-086-9, 128 pp, $5.95

Quiet Places with Mary
Isaias Powers, CP
The 24 guided meditations in this book are directed to living life in
the presence of God, as revealed by Jesus, with Mary as a companion.

ISBN: 0-89622-297-7, 160 pp, $5.95

I Am a Pilgrim Child
Carolyn Deitering
By recounting moments from her own childhood, the author helps
us get in touch with the child within each of us.

ISBN: 0-89622-499-6, 80 pp, $7.95

Available at religious bookstores or from
TWENTY-THIRD PUBLICATIONS
P.O. Box 180 • Mystic, CT 06355
1-800-321-0411